Everyday

Stephanie Nixon

www.apostles-publishing.com

FAITHBUILDERS

Everyday Miracles by Stephanie Nixon

First Published in Great Britain in 2019

Apostolos Publishing Ltd,
3rd Floor, 207 Regent Street,
London W1B 3HH

www.apostolos-publishing.com

A catalog record for this book is available from the British Library

ISBN: 978-1-912120-11-6

Cover Design by Apostolos Publishing Ltd. Cover Image © Lilkar | Dreamstime.com

Printed and bound in Great Britain by Marston Book Services Limited, Oxfordshire.

Contents

Foreword

This project was born out of a spark of inspiration at a prayer meeting at my local Christian Centre, where a senior church member stated that, "We should talk more about the miracles that happen in our lives."

There was more to this than a spark of inspiration, and after saying my prayers, and asking God to guide me, I reached out to others to share their stories, and this book was produced.

Everyday Miracles is a collection of fifty miracle stories from ordinary people who want to share the good news about the miracles God has done for them, praying that it will encourage you and give you hope as you face problems and needs in your own life.

Each miracle is a testimony of faith in God, the power prayer has, and how God works in the lives of everyone. Just call Him, pray to him and He will answer in the most wonderful of ways.

"For nothing will be impossible with God." Luke 1:37

All proceeds from sales will go to the Lorna Byrne Children's Foundation.

Acknowledgments

This book would not have been possible if it was not for all of those who have kindly contributed their testimonies. So, a massive thank you to everyone who shared their miracle stories!

A special thanks to Pastor John, from the Acocks Green Christian Centre, who inspired me to write this book following a prayer meeting where the subject was raised.

Many thanks to Mavis Mundirwa, my writing coach, for guiding me and advising me with her expertise.

Many thanks also to Mathew, the director of Apostolos Publishing, for his ongoing support, and for making this ambition a reality. Many thanks also to the members of my family who shared their miracles!

I also thank God for giving me the courage and guidance to do this book. All glory and praise to Him!

This book presents the testimonies of a wonderful mixture of miracles from people of all walks of Christian faith, meeting God in the most wondrous of ways, demonstrating the wonderful work of God in individuals' lives! Many of these incidents may seem small or insignificant, and may not even be considered "miraculous," but they meant a lot to those who experienced them. Whether great or small, they were ordinary, everyday "miracles" for us!

Everyday Miracles Project Coordinator: Stephanie Violet Nixon

God Took Away My Childhood Depression

I remember it as if it only happened yesterday. When I was thirteen years old, I had my first profound spiritual experience. Looking back (though it was never mentioned at the time) I realize now that I was experiencing quite terrible childhood depression. Every night I had raging storms in my head; I could not sleep well at all. I remember that I was constantly on edge, upset and angry. I was frequently tearful, especially as I could not sleep, I dreaded having to wake up and go to school the next day.

I cannot remember exactly how long this went on for, except that it was for months on end. I could not see any way to break out of this vicious cycle. Every night was the same for me; crying in a distressed state for hours. Both my parents worried about me as they did not know what to do. They had tried everything to help me get through this, and nothing was working. I cannot remember what caused the depression, but somehow, I found myself trapped in the cycle of being upset, distressed and angry for no reason at all.

From my earliest days, my family and I were practicing Christians. I remember praying with my mum that God would help me get through this, that I might have a better night's sleep, and that the terrible thoughts and storms in my head would go away. One night she laid her hands on my head and prayed. I prayed hard too; I begged the Lord to take away my pain, and I offered up my suffering to Him so he could use it for His will.

I prayed hard for months. I was taught as a child that by offering up my sufferings, God would use them for good and that one day I could help others who needed healing and comfort. That gave me a sense of peace knowing that by offering up my own suffering, God would use it to help others. I prayed every night that God would give me peace and to take away the pain that I was experiencing, and that He might use my suffering.

Then one day I woke up and it was all gone! I felt this overwhelming sense of peace and contentment and was overflowing with an indescribable joy. The pain that I carried for months had gone, and it was replaced with abundant joy and happiness! It was also the most unusual experience of my life. I had been carrying a burden on my shoulders for months, and suddenly my body was as light as a feather.

My gratitude was immeasurable. God had taken my suffering from me and had filled me with joy and peace. This profound spiritual experience taught me about the power of prayer and the power of offering my sufferings up to God. God took away my childhood depression overnight.

Stephanie Violet Nixon

Rock Bottom

I remember the moment I hit rock bottom. I was standing at the sink in my small kitchen and staring at the dirty dishes. With no central heating, and a boiler that took two hours to warm up enough to provide hot water, I had to boil the kettle to fill up the sink to cope with the washing up. I would wash up twice on Sundays when there were more pans than usual, but most days the washing up consisted of a couple of cups and plates and several baby bottles.

As I waited for the kettle to boil, my mind began going around in circles, and my stomach twisted with anxiety until it felt as though I had knots forming right up into my throat. Things were hard. No, things were quite desperate.

When the baby was born, I left work. The boss had phoned me to ask if I would come back, which was a lovely compliment and I did miss adult conversation, but I would never leave my baby. She was beautiful. So small and so dependent. I loved her so completely! I couldn't imagine how I could ever leave her care to the hands of others. The only problem was losing half our income. The bigger half. This not only meant things were hard, but they were also well near impossible!

The items on the sink were not doing so well at distracting me today. Keeping busy wasn't distracting me from the hopelessness I was feeling. The baby was asleep at last, so now, I could cry alone without worrying she would pick up the "sad mummy" vibes from me.

My husband and I didn't own a car. We didn't go on holidays, have any loans or credit cards. We didn't go out for meals or treats. We didn't buy new clothes. We simply lived, breathed, and loved. These were the most basic things needed to survive but living even on the basics was draining all the income. Feeding ourselves meant a carefully crafted trip to the supermarket. Our budget was enough to ensure we ate, but not enough to add taste or joy to mealtimes.

I didn't know how long we could go on. It was hard on my husband who worked so much. It was barely manageable. If there was a birthday for a niece or nephew, the money that went into the card seemed to leave a hole twice its size in our budget.

As I stared out of the window, the sun was shining; but I didn't feel its warmth. The grass needed cutting, but I had no energy. There was a breeze as trees were swaying gently, but I found no comfort in nature as I usually would.

I had tried to become like my baby, where all she needed was a roof over her head, food, and to be loved. The material things didn't matter to her, and so they shouldn't have mattered to me. She didn't care if her clothes arrived in a bag from a friend's child who no longer needed them. Why should I care? My daughter was beautiful no matter what she wore. And I was always grateful. It was only a kind of gentle snobbery that makes us think we need to give a child brand-label clothes. We can do the best for them without handing over large sums of money to clothe them.

I had a two-pence piece in my purse and a passport-sized photo of my husband and me from before we were married; before I learned how to shape my eyebrows! The picture was a happy one full of love, but the two-pence was a reminder of the hardships.

The kettle tremored in its final boil and clicked off. I grabbed the washing up liquid bottle and squeezed it upside down into the sink. A hiss of escaping air and two bubbles popped at the nozzle. I shook it and tried again. I had thought I had some left, but clearly, I was wrong.

That was the moment I hit rock bottom when I realized that I didn't even have enough money to buy washing up liquid. Flipping washing up liquid! The most basic of things.

The tears washed down my face then and I sobbed. I stared through blurry vision to the fuzzy looking clouds in the sky.

I had hit the despair of rock bottom and seeing no way out.

"God help me," I cried. I bowed my head and cried a little more quietly. I juddered a breath and raised my eyes again to the clouds. "I need your help. I can't cope. I'm trying, trying to do it, but it is so hard. I know you have always provided, like with someone turning up with clothes, and I love that and thank you for helping them to think of me, but we are struggling. I'm sorry I haven't the strong faith to know it will all be alright. I'm sorry that I doubt. I need help. Please, can you help me? Us. Some little sign. Anything. I know I shouldn't ask, and I know I don't deserve it, and that I should put my faith and trust in you, but it is so hard right now. I am struggling. I can't see a way out. I can't leave my baby and go to work. That would break me. You gave me a child … please help me … help me stay here to love and raise her. I don't want to be rich, but we just need some help as we are desperate. Things are hard. I know it is harder for others, but it is hard for my little family. I am sorry, Lord. I love you. Please help me."

I prayed with all my heart and soul. I remember being aware of the warmth from the sun on my face and the lightness of the blue sky as I wiped away at the tears.

And then I heard the flap of the letterbox and the post hit the hall floor.

I felt dread hit my stomach. I didn't want it to be a brown envelope – an unexpected bill. That would really be the icing on the cake; though I felt beyond that point already. It wasn't my birthday, so no cards with money which we desperately needed.

I wiped my hands and shuffled into the hall. The baby was still asleep. There was an advertising type of flyer on the floor, full of color that seemed to mock my drab hall. A company had bought out a new product or something. I didn't especially care and knew I wouldn't be able to buy whatever it was anyway, but I opened it up.

It was advertising a new product, the launch of a new fragrance – and inside was a coupon for a free sample … of washing up liquid.

I almost dropped to my knees and began to cry again, but this time for a whole other reason.

God already had things in hand. He knew the right time and place to set things in motion so that the answer came at exactly the right moment. The sign, if you like, that I needed. The little miracle. The one thing right then that I needed most to get me through that day, and to lift my spirits so high, I felt like I could touch heaven and feel the love pouring out over me and sweeping through my soul, nourishing it.

Holding that voucher, I knew at that moment, with every part of my being, that everything would be okay. I was being watched over and looked after. My prayer had been heard and my family was being protected. No matter how hard it got, it would always work out one way or another for the best of my soul. I would draw on the strength that came from my faith and be supported when it waned. No, I would never be rich. No, I may never have what I wanted, but would always receive exactly what I needed – even if my heart didn't know it yet or in which shape or form it would be presented.

To every other person receiving that leaflet through their door, it would look like a voucher for a free bottle of washing up liquid. For me, it was a miracle – an answer to a prayer. A confirmation that God is watching and waiting for us to ask for his help. He is eager to help because he loves us so much. Sometimes, we must hit rock bottom before we really feel the need to turn to him and seek his support. But our gratitude is magnified when we receive the answer to our prayers. When God answers the needs and worries of our heart, which only he can see, we feel like children again. Children with a loving heavenly parent who cares for our every need. When we pray and ask for help, we give God the chance to show us how much he loves us.

I was so full of joy that day, and for many days to come. No matter how hard it became, I thought of that voucher – that day. We are never alone in our struggles or worries. To those who are still trying to go it alone, you only need to turn to God, ask his help, and his will shall be done in the form of little miracles you could never see coming and which will take your breath away when they happen.

Never let fear conquer. Never give up hope. Always pray; ask for help.

And that day, I had one more prayer I needed to say from the heart, and quickly as my tiny girl had just woken and sounded hungry.

"Thank you, my Lord and my God. Thank you for loving me."

Juliette

The Shadow

I was exhausted, we all were. It had been a long day of playgroup, pre-school nursery, and school for my little ones and me. We had to make several journeys that day as we did every day. But today I seemed to be more tired. My 3-year-old twins were holding onto the handlebars of the double buggy and I could feel their weight dragging me until my back ached. The baby in the left seat was awake and ready for a feed, and my toddler was squirming in her seat harness, wanting to get out. My eldest daughter was walking along the top of a small wall by the petrol station we passed, and I was trying to encourage her to jump down and stay close so that we could cross the entrance together while I kept an eye out for cars pulling in. There were many main roads to cross and not enough crossings between school and home, and the last stretch was uphill.

My legs were heavy, and I could have dropped to the pavement and slept right there. There were only three hundred yards to our home, but it seemed like miles and I struggled. I seemed to have no strength or energy left that day after the previous night disturbed by feeds and potty training. The day's routine was the same as any other, but I was too physically and emotionally drained to cope. The nights were drawing in and, in the distance, I could already see the sun lowering on the other side of the hill. I just wanted to make it home before it got dark.

I suddenly became aware of my thoughts and felt self-pity stirring inside, and then tried to shake myself out of it. But it wasn't working.

"God," I thought, "I'm exhausted. My little ones are tired and only have little legs. It's been a long day. Please give us the strength to get home. Please let time pass quickly and get us to our door."

My legs were so heavy.

"Please help, God ..." and then I seemed too tired to even think for a moment.

I tried to focus. I had to get us home but wanted to make it enjoyable for the children. If only we could find the energy to go a little faster, so we could all rest at home and I could take a few moments before starting the tea and feeds. I often sang nursery rhymes with them, or played an alphabet animal guessing game, but wasn't sure I had the energy to do any of that today.

"Help me, give me strength."

There was only one other person on the pavement ahead of us, a man so far ahead that if I knew his name and shouted it he wouldn't have heard me. And that was when I noticed his shadow.

"Look at that man's shadow!" I said to the children. "That is the biggest shadow I have ever seen!"

And it was! It stretched all the way from the man to the wheels of the pushchair as the sun was now so low, but still shining in our faces. It was the length of ten houses.

"It is so long!" I said. "Imagine how long our shadows must be. Let's look!"

And my children and I turned around to look, but we cast no shadows. I paused for a moment. There was only dark pavement. I didn't understand. I looked forward at the sun, and then at the man's long shadow ending at the pavement right in front of the wheels, then looked back. We didn't have any shadows.

My little family was right on the point where darkness and light met. On the very edge of day and night. And yet the sun was on my face.

I looked back again and then felt such joy and peace fill through me. I felt renewed vigor and strength as if it was a gift suddenly handed to me. It was almost as if God was holding on to nature so that we were kept in the light to guide us home.

"Come on, let's beat the shadows home."

I felt my heart lighten, as strength and energy filled my body and the aches and pains seemed to diminish. We all quickened our pace as if rejuvenated, and I glanced back often to see nothing but the dark pavement. We crossed the last road as the sun lowered but still filtered through the trees and kept on until we reached home with it still on our faces. And then we turned onto our front garden and up to the doorstep where I reached for my keys. I looked back at the pavement.

"Look at that!" I said to the children.

We saw the darkness move across the pavement in front of us. The light turning to dark. It seemed to roll past like a foreboding dark wave, but we were home, the front door was open, and the three older ones piled in to take their shoes off.

I stood on the step for a moment longer, watching as the evening rolled in further along the street as the sun finally sunk behind the trees and was just a scattering of light within seconds.

It was a wonderful little miracle for my family to see, a prayer answered at the moment we needed it which gave strength and encouragement. We had been right on the edge of night and day, but we remained in the light until we got home.

"Thank you," I whispered, then closed the door on the night.

Juliette

A Miracle from Prayer, Faith, and Tears

At the local Servite Convent, one of the sisters, Hilda, decided to start a prayer group for mothers whose children attended the Servite School of Our Lady of Compassion. The school was for infants and juniors, and it was felt that this was a way to deepen the faith of the young mums, helping them on their spiritual journey.

It was decided to hold the group at the Convent every Wednesday evening and many mums came, including me, to listen and pray together. One of the regular mums was Joan. She had three sons, the youngest being only three years old. Joan and I were great friends and often had a coffee together. Slowly, Joan began to become unwell with terrible headaches, and one day, her husband noticed that she was not coordinating properly, so she visited the doctors.

After further investigations, it was discovered that she had a serious brain tumor. The doctors allowed her to return home to sort out affairs, such as prepare a will, etc. because the operation she needed presented a great risk to her life. The mums from our little group, including Sister Hilda, supported the family, making sure the children were going to be looked after, at school and at home, giving the husband time to be with her.

The day before she went into hospital happened to be a Wednesday, so we persuaded her to come to the prayer group that evening. Joan loved the prayer group and it seemed natural to have her with us to pray for her recovery. We were all overcome as we prayed, and tears flowed because we realized it may be the last time we saw her. Our prayers were real, and suddenly, Sister Hilda got up and gently placed her hands on Joan's head. She stood there for a few minutes gently praying over her, and we all shed more tears. We took Joan home and waited.

As I was looking after her three-year-old, I had contact with Joan's husband, but then one morning, I got a call from Joan herself! She was deliriously happy saying that when they had gone in to remove the tumor, it had disappeared! The consultant said it was a "million to one" chance of this ever happening, and that he could not understand why, after all the X-rays and scans, it was no longer there. "It must be a miracle!"

I cried over the phone and agreed that something must have happened when Sister Hilda placed her hands on her. To my joy, Joan told me that when she placed her hands on her that Wednesday night, she felt a rushing of water in her head. It was not an unpleasant feeling, but she felt frightened not knowing what had happened to her. She decided not to say anything to us at that time, not knowing what the outcome would be.

What joy I felt! I believe this was a miracle. The faith of Sister Hilda and the other mums was heard in Heaven, and God gave His answer and healed Joan. I went to tell Sister Hilda, who was very humble about it all. This little miracle will always be in our hearts knowing that God hears the prayers from his sincere and faithful children.

Joan still had to recover from the big operation which cut into her skull, but she was soon back looking after her children and thanking God for her life.

Rosie Jane

Presence of God

When I was younger, I gave evidence against my child abuser, who got off on the historical charges against me and another woman on a technicality, despite the Crown Prosecution Service lawyer saying I was one of the best live witnesses he'd ever seen in such circumstances.

I went home and made the calm decision to kill myself. It wasn't spontaneous – I cleaned the whole house, so the police wouldn't think badly of me when they found me. I applied to my insurance company and changed my next of kin with the forms that I had to wait to arrive in the post. I did the gardening.

I wrote handover notes for all my files at work. I put all my documents in order and made a will. It took about a week to get everything in order. I was calm and logical about it. I had decided what I was going to do and wasn't distressed because I had a plan and had decided that I just didn't want to live in a world of injustice any longer. I had no belief in God at this point and had been raised as an atheist.

I cleaned the last cupboard. Finished the last thing I had to do before I could finally leave my unwanted life. As I thought with a sense of relief that I could finally end it, I said to myself "it's time." No sooner had I thought it than this unexplainable sense of someone being there and this totally overwhelming wave of their love and security washed over me.

I felt a very real and physical presence around me with a power I find hard to describe. I knew something bigger than me had me in their care. It carried me through. I don't subscribe to every bit of the Bible, but the best explanation I have of my experience is that it was God, and today my faith in his existence is totally unshakable – because I felt it.

I have subsequently read the poem "Footprints," and it sums up for me the way I was carried through something I couldn't handle alone.

Jennifer

My Spiritual Journey

I was taking the "Rite of Christian Initiation of Adults," for adult converts to Catholicism, and I was asked to tell the story of my spiritual journey. This was in 1993.

In his book "Conversations with God," Neale Walsch asks God the question, "How do I know that my conversations with you are not just my imagination?" God replies, "Would that make a difference if it were? I can communicate with you through your imagination just as easily as by any other means. Mine is always your highest thought, your clearest word, your grandest feeling. Anything less is from another source."

My Story

I cannot remember when I first became religious. Even as a small child I believed in God, but I saw him like a spoiling parent and asked him for material things of a frivolous nature. Like many children, I hated Sunday school and would do all sorts of things to avoid it.

My mother was a religious person and over the years became more involved in the church. Out of a family of five well-spaced children, I appeared to be the only one to follow her in search for a greater meaning and, mysteriously, the only one named after an evangelist (Saint Mark) and an apostle (Andrew is my middle name).

I was a bit confused as a child because my mother suffered from a mental disorder. At times things were good and she looked after me well. But since she favored my younger brother, when things were not so good, I was the unlucky one who copped the abuse. In spite of the favoritism, I loved my brother and was happy for him. He and I grew very close. Even to the point that when I was away in the army, if he needed me he seemed to be able to call me and I would feel a compulsion to go home.

He was very well liked in the community for his care and concern for others. He once went to the Melbourne Show by bus with a friend. When his friend became ill he cared for him for the whole day, missing all the things he went to see. Neighbors and friends knew their children were safe whenever he was asked to keep an eye on them.

One day our eyes met for a moment and I felt like I was looking into the eyes of the Lord. As he turned to leave, I wanted to call him back but felt paralyzed somehow. So off he went to do what he loved most, riding his motorbike. He never returned.

After my brother's death, my mother's mental suffering intensified, and I too had my own cross to bear. I had been from drug to drug and psychiatrist to psychiatrist trying to find even a moment's respite from the demon illness that tortured my brain. For the first forty years of my life, I felt just like the Israelites – I was in the wilderness.

Although I believed in God, I could not seem to contact him; in my suffering, there were times when I cursed him. Like St Paul, I was amongst the foremost sinners. But Jesus never stopped loving me. As a mature man, I can now see how he carried me through all the difficult times. At my lowest ebb, like Christ himself who fell and lacked the strength to rise, I cried out and I could hear his voice directly in my mind saying, "Trust in me, my son."

I think that this was when my trust and love for him began. When I look back on my life, I can see how he has been true to his word. Although life hasn't been easy, he has always seen to it that my burdens have not been too great for my strength. In the Bible, he said believe in me and I will give you abundant life. I wanted a wife and children. He gave them to me. I wanted a nice house for them. He gave that too.

Becoming unemployed through my illness I felt it would be impossible to ever regain employment, but then became well enough to work and applied for a job. Even though I messed up the interview, I was still accepted. Ironically, I learned later that my interviewer was an active Christian. Life could have been really awful without Jesus carrying me through the difficult times and reminding me of his love for me.

I had been raised as an Anglican, but my wife was a Catholic and our children were being brought up through the Catholic school system. We went to Mass together at St. Mary's. I had developed a great love of this house of God because I could not forget the strong aura of peace that I had felt from the first time I had entered it, even though I had only come to repair the organ and did not even have religion in mind. Eventually, a prominent Catholic women's league lady, Molly Jensen, somehow noticed me and asked me if I would like to become a Catholic. I entered the church through the RCIA process. I cannot forget the rite of acceptance. I was asked if I was nervous in front of all those people? I replied, "How could you feel afraid when you felt as though Christ was cradling you in his arms?"

In the meantime, my mother, now in her seventies, had deteriorated physically. In her later years, she had sacrificed a lot for me to help hold my marriage together while I battled with my illness. I visited her often and she would say, "Hello Mark," even before she could have known it was me. I would make the sign of the cross on her forehead and tell her to be patient that he will be coming for her soon. But her suffering appeared to continue endlessly.

I wondered what I was supposed to do. Could it be that I was expected to end it for her? But no, somehow, I just knew that something important was happening. Mother appeared to be evolving into something special. One day she asked me if Norelle, my daughter, was alright now, as she had heard her scream. I remembered that Norelle had driven a staple into her finger and had cried out in pain that morning.

Mother appeared to be reaching out of the tomb that was her body. Then one day she died. I felt disappointed because I was sure that because of our faith that I would have felt something special when she went. But no, she was dead and that was that, and I had not even been with her when she went. Some months later, at a Mass for the confirmation of grade 6 children, something truly wonderful happened. I felt a tingling sensation on my forehead.

Very slowly it moved down stopping just above my nose, then it started again above the eye and moved across. This was unmistakably the sign of the cross. This event puzzled me as I had never experienced anything like it before. It was nearly a week later while riding my bike and meditating that the penny dropped. This was what I used to do to mother! Dare I believe that she had reached from the grave to make the sign of the cross on my forehead?

If it were possible, and even if there were some penalty for doing it, I have no doubt that my mother would do it for me. I remember her telling me one time that she did not want me to be spending my spare time coming to see her. She would rather that I go and enjoy myself. My reply was that if we only looked after ourselves and did not care about each other, then there could be no love in the world and I could not live in a world like that.

My only explanation for this event was that I had given her one of the greatest gifts that Jesus had come to earth to teach. Forgiveness! And the sign of the cross brought with it the message that in doing so, I had been forgiven for my sins also. At the Easter Vigil and my First Communion, I wondered if I would have any other experiences of the Spirit and I did. I looked at the eyes of the five hundred people loving and welcoming me and through them, I saw the face of Christ in his people, his body! I felt truly at home. Shortly after this my son and other students underwent their confirmation.

My mother had been a Sunday school teacher for many years, and such an occasion would have been special to her. I wondered if I would feel the sign of the cross again, and I did. This time I felt it the entire length and width of my face and in the years to come, feeling the sign of the cross became a regular occurrence.

Part 2: 16 years later −2009

Sometimes I have felt that thoughts which came into my head were not my own, just like the first when I had heard the Lord tell me to trust in him. On my first trip to East Timor, saddened by the intense suffering of these beautiful people, I stood below a concrete cross on a hill above Dili and mused to myself, "Why wouldn't you put an end to such suffering?" Instantly into my mind, I heard a voice. "Many souls would be lost if I did it now."

A new drug had given me some years of peace from my illness, and so I had the fantastic experience of being able to teach English to students in East Timor. But the effects of the medication were starting to wane and even worse some new and horrible symptoms were starting to emerge.

On one occasion when I was scheduled to do a talk at RCIA, I had been in a state of anxiety due to changes in medication and its withdrawal effects. I wondered if I should use a tranquillizer to calm me so that I would be able to do it properly and not embarrass myself. But I kept thinking I needed to show my trust and faith in Jesus by not using it. Just before the talk a thought suddenly came into my mind, "You don't have to be a Martyr Mark, I know how much you love me." So I took the tranquillizer and had a great time. The talk was on the Eucharist and the following Sunday I was an Extraordinary Minister of the Eucharist and I had the most powerful sense of the presence of Jesus. So even if my talk was a bit off, at least Jesus still loves me.

Things started to get worse with my illness, the last resort drug which had helped for several months had failed and I was experiencing some nasty feelings. We had our house on the market as we had planned to build again, which would keep me occupied, but just at the critical time we found a buyer and had to find a place quickly, so we could move out.

This was an enormous task because of all my tools and equipment. But despite some terrible anxiety we managed to get settled. I'm sure it was thanks to the help of Jesus that a comfortable home with an enormous shed came along just at the right time. But my condition continued to deteriorate. I had often wondered if hearing the voice of Jesus coaching me had been real or just my imagination. Then came the clincher!

When all medical treatment had failed, and I was suffering intensely, I lay down in a most horrible state of depression. I felt my burden too heavy to bear. I wished with all my soul for death to envelop me, so I could slip away peacefully. In my mind, I heard a gentle voice say, "If you went now Mark, you would be very disappointed that you gave up so easily." Finally realizing that it was the medication that was the problem, I started the painful withdrawal process.

Through my recovery, whenever I closed my eyes and thought about Jesus, I would feel the sign of the cross on my forehead, reminding me of God's love, and of the love of my mother and brother.

Mark Owen

Healing: My Little Sister

I remember it as if it were yesterday. My little sister was two years old and she had a large knot in the soft tissue under her chin. It felt like an egg. The doctor had no idea what it was, but scheduled surgery to remove it. I was eight years old and my mum asked me to help her pray for healing. We had never done such a thing before, but we held hands and put our arms around my baby sister. The next morning the lump was gone and the tissue under her chin was normal.

Healing: My Mother

My Mum endured fifteen years of periodically waking around 4 am with mouth, tongue and throat swelling. She was rushed to the hospital many times and was eventually sent to a specialist in another part of the country for allergy tests.

She only showed minor reactions to the things she consumed almost daily, such as tea. So finally, they kept her overnight under observation and it happened there. She had what they called an idiopathic allergic reaction because they had no idea what caused it. My mum desperately started praying for healing from this condition, and I'm happy to say it hasn't happened since. She has been free from this for at least ten years. She's now eighty-nine years old and in great health.

Gwendolyn Lee

An Encounter with an Angel

18th June 2016 was a beautiful day. I was driving back from a museum in Los Angeles, where we'd had my daughter's 15th birthday pictures taken. When I suddenly got a flat tire, I pulled over to the emergency lane, put my emergency lights on before setting to work changing the tire.

A passing motorist fell asleep at the wheel and headed right into us, pinning me between my car and his. I instantly had both legs amputated by the crash. Out of nowhere, my three daughters saw a man run up to me and start CPR. He took the belt off his pants and made a tourniquet for my leg. He saved my life.

When the ambulance came, the girls looked up and wanted to thank the man who saved my life – but he had vanished. They say they never saw a car pull up – he appeared out of nowhere and just as mysteriously he had left. I was in the hospital in a coma for three months. In the coma, I dreamt of my brother, my father, and all the other members of my family who had died before me. I saw them in a cloud far away from me.

They say I died three times and came back. When I awoke, I could remember nothing about the accident – to this day all I remember is my daughter's photo shoot. I awoke from the coma calm, and thankful God had let me live to see my children grow up. And I now even have three beautiful grandchildren! God has truly blessed me. He touched me in so many ways. I am truly blessed because of him.

Linda Del Toro

Holy Fire Miracle

It was Easter, and Father Tim had been sharing with me about the Easter Fire. One team had previously gone to Saint Nicholas Church in Oxford to receive the Easter Fire (also called "Holy Fire"). On the way back, it sadly went out. Father Tim explained that we would go the following week and try again. I was excited, I couldn't wait! But I hadn't really understood what the Holy Fire was about, being so new to Orthodoxy. So when I arrived home I chatted with Father Tim who sent me some links to YouTube videos. Now I was even more excited.

The Holy Fire descends into the Tomb of Christ in the Holy Sepulchre church in Jerusalem during Easter week. The flame appears in a closed tomb and is carried into a massively crowded church. The flame is cool and doesn't burn, and now sent around the world to different countries as a sign of unity.

The following Saturday, we left for Oxford. We stayed for Vespers on Saturday and then collected the Holy Fire. We delivered the Fire first to St Anne's in Northampton and then to our reader's house before mine.

On Sunday I woke early to check the Holy Fire was still alight. It was and so I promptly told Father Tim all was good. He asked me to bring it to the church in case the Fire had gone out at church.

I lit a candle from my main fire and proceeded to my front door. I opened the stepped out and left. Instantly the wind came and blew out my candle. I fumbled for my door keys, opened my door and stepped through. As I did so the candle reignited instantly.

I screamed with excitement. At the time I hadn't realized that I had awoken my wife. My two youngest daughters who were awake came running. "What happened?" they asked.

"God re-lit my candle," I explained.

"What God lit your candle by Himself?"

"Yes," I said and left again.

Again, the wind blew out my candle, and I fumbled for my keys and opened the door. Once more as I stepped through my door it reignited.

This time my kids were still trying to work out what happened and so were close to the door and one said she saw it re-light.

This would have been around 08:45 as I wanted to arrive at St Anne's in time to re-light the candle in the church if needed. I was so excited I was close to exploding.

I arrived at St Anne's and had to tell Father James. As I finished Father Tim walked in and again, I could not contain myself or my excitement about what had happened.

Within a week I had gone from not knowing about the Holy Fire from Jerusalem to having witnessed what was, for me, my own little Easter miracle.

Thank you, God; I am still excited about it.

Christopher (Compo) Baker

The Miracle of Faith

Although I was educated at Olton Court Convent, I was not a Catholic. One day, about thirty-three years ago, I decided to go and see what Benediction was all about. I drove up to the Friary, but it was in darkness, and there were no other cars in the car park. Deciding that I had got my day or time wrong, I left.

I was coming back around the roundabout to go down Kineton Green Road when I suddenly felt my steering wheel pulling back towards St. Bernard's Road where the Friary is (the local Catholic church).

I found myself, again, at the Friary. It was still all in darkness, but someone tapped on the window and asked if I was okay. I said I wanted to go to the Benediction, so the lady who tapped on the window told me to park up and go with her.

The Benediction was not held in the church, but in the chapel round the back where the Sacred Heart Fathers lived. That night I was going back home, but God had other ideas, and they say the rest is history!

Perhaps we need to listen to the Holy Spirit more!

Ros Sherman

Little Miracle

My husband and I have six children and we decided to go to Wales for a short holiday. Owing to a trapped nerve in my back, I was unable to sit down as the pain was too great.

We decided to send three of the older children down by train, so the rest could lie in the back of our estate car for the long journey. For the return journey after the holiday, my youngest son (who was only six years old) wanted to go with his big brother and sister on the train. I was very unhappy about this, but my husband said it would be fine, so I reluctantly said yes.

It made me very tearful and emotional as my husband took them to board the train. I could see that it was packed and there seemed to be no room at all for them at all to sit. The journey back was three or four hours, too long for a six-year-old to stand.

My husband didn't have time to find a seat for them, so we had no idea if they found a seat as the train started off, and my husband had to get off the crowded train.

As I lay in the back of the car, I thought what poor parents we were for not being able to seat them on the train before we started our journey in the car. My tears were real as we started our journey home. I felt helpless as I lay in the back of the car and prayed that they would be alright.

Suddenly, the car pulled to a stop at the railway junction from which the railway crossed over to go on its way. We waited and as I looked out of the window from my lying position, I suddenly saw the train passing over the junction.

What joy! On the train, sitting by the window, was my six-year-old son and the older children!

What a wonderful miracle this was for our car to be at the junction at the precise moment to see my son and put my mind to rest. Then I cried with joy and gave thanks to God for this little miracle. My son even caught sight of me in the back of the car and gave a little wave. Praise the Lord!

Jane Wareing

Visit from the Grave

It was June/July 2017, and I had been bereft twice within the space of a couple of weeks. Mid-June one of my lecturers and former employers had passed away from pneumonia and I was heartbroken. I attended his funeral later that week and was continuing life as normal.

It was only a few weeks later that one of my former students died of throat cancer. He was young, full of ambition, and wanted to make something of his life. A few weeks previously, the university reported that he had completed his degree, and had a private graduation, for which I was so overjoyed.

He suffered from his illness throughout his degree, but his faith in God and love of life inspired him to persist despite these obstacles. I was his note taker at the university and loved the gentle and kind way he had with people. When the news came of his death, it was in the university newsletter. I was devastated. The newsletter showed his beautiful smiling face holding up his degree certificate, in his elegant graduation gown. Tears rolled down my face, and I was comforted by my sister who gave me a big hug.

For the following few weeks, my heart was heavy, and I struggled to come to terms with his death. I found myself somewhat withdrawn as I struggled with the bereavement. I was constantly thinking about him and praying. I could not stop thinking about why this wonderful young man who was so gentle and tender towards everyone he met, and who was so content and full of life despite his circumstances, had gone so suddenly.

One afternoon, I was alone at home; I went upstairs to my bedroom, and I felt he was there. As in a vision, my student was stood at the end of the room, dressed in his graduation gown, smiling at me. He said to me *"thank you for helping me."* He turned and walked into a golden white light behind him and was gone. More warm tears rolled down my face, and I thank God for sending this vision to console me, giving me closure and to heal my heart from the bereavement. My student has inspired many others through his persistence, love of life and will to overcome all barriers despite the odds against him.

Anonymous

My Out of Body Experience with Jesus

I have sleep apnoea. One night many years ago when I was asleep, I must have stopped breathing, for I suddenly found myself at a place I had never seen before. It was a very peaceful and beautiful place. The first thing I remember seeing was about five or six very old men dressed in white robes.

They were sitting leisurely on benches at what I can only describe as an outdoor Greek portico with lovely columns and having an open ceiling. They said nothing to me but were watching me rather quizzically, as if trying to understand who I was and what I was doing there.

Then my attention was diverted to my left by a dazzling white brilliance and I was both overjoyed and amazed to be standing face to face with my Lord and Savior Jesus Christ! My Lord said to me, "This isn't your time, you must go back," and I immediately awakened.

I now know why He sent me back. Prior to this, I had never written anything, but since then I have published sixteen books and hope to have my seventeenth published soon. Twelve of the books contain my Christian poems.

John McKee

Train Journey to Clacton

When I was a seven-year-old lad my mother, father, younger brother and I were having a week's holiday in Clacton, traveling from the London suburb of Sudbury Hill. My dad had decided to get a very early train from Liverpool Street. We were awoken at 5:30 in the morning and took the Underground to the mainline station.

My dad bought the tickets and we went to catch the 7:35 train. Luckily, we found a compartment with no one in it and took our seats. The guard arrived and looked at the tickets and explained to my dad that seat reservations were needed for the train we were on.

We all got off the train and my brother and I sat down rather despondently on a luggage trolley, the smoke and steam from the locomotive was billowing around us and out of this smoke the silhouette of a man appeared, he walked towards, very smartly dressed and wearing a trilby hat, as many men did at the time.

He approached my dad and said, "My friends and I were going to catch this train, but they have obviously been delayed, here, please take my reservations and catch this train." We took them and thanked him and boarded the train just as the guard's whistle went and the train started to pull away from the platform.

I looked out of the window for the man, but he was nowhere in sight. To a young boy of my age, the whole thing seemed an absolute miracle!

Chris Clavey

My First Time at Youth Camp

When I was twelve years old, and my mum was about to give birth to my sister, both mum and dad asked if I wanted to go on holiday by myself to a Church of England holiday camp for boys and girls aged 12–15 in Seasalter near Whitstable in Kent. I had never been away by myself before, yet without knowing a single person at the camp I reluctantly said yes. The day finally arrived (it was a Saturday) and I went to the coach pick up point. Each person could take £2 in pocket money, but I had no savings and my parents could only manage to give me £1.

We were a middle-class family living in a London suburb, quite comfortable in a lot of respects, but because there was only one wage coming into the house there wasn't an awful lot of spare money after the mortgage and bills were paid.

I was the only person in a dormitory of fifteen boys who did not hand over the full two pounds to the bursar. Even the eleven rough and ready lads from Poplar on the Isle of Dogs had the full complement of money. These were pre-decimal days when the currency was pounds, shillings, and pence.

We got to Wednesday and thanks to the local seaside attractions, such as the wonderful sweet shop, ice cream parlor, and boating lake, I only had four shillings and sixpence left. The two friends I had made wanted to take the bus into Faversham the next day. I just about had enough money to pay the bus fares and get my mum a small present but that would have left me short of money for the last full day and the coach journey home.

My friend Edwin asked if I wanted to take a canoe out on the boating lake if we shared the hire fee, I reluctantly agreed but explained to him that I wouldn't be able to go to Faversham the next day and would hang around the camp. We went down to the boating lake and enjoyed our half an hour in the canoe, our other friend also had a boat, so we pretended to be pirates attacking another ship, a great game involving some splashing.

The boat owner had just told us we were on our last five minutes when a man appeared on the path next to the lake. He was dressed in old clothes and his trousers were done up with string. I recall that he also looked extremely grubby, like a chimney sweep but that he had kind blue eyes.

The man shouted to us, "Hey boys!" and started throwing silver coins from his coat pockets onto the path. He did not stop walking, leave a small trail of coins in his wake, some bounced and landed in the water. Edwin and I jumped out of our canoe and waded the short distance to shore, both immediately scrambling to get the coins, when there were none left on the path I jumped back in the lake and picked up the few coins in there too.

The man had continued to walk along the oxbow path around the lake, occasionally turning and smiling and laughing at us. By the time I had got out of the water and shouted my thanks again he had got to the furthest point on the path from us and disappeared. Edwin and I jumped back in the water to retrieve the canoe and paddles so that we didn't incur the wrath of the boat owner and spoil what was turning out to be a rather wonderful day.

We lay on the grass in the park by the boating lake and let the sun dry our clothes I counted my new wealth and had gained seven shillings and sixpence, making the money in my pocket eleven shillings, just over half of what I had started with on Saturday. The next day we went to Faversham, had tea and cakes in a café, I bought myself a book on steam locomotives that I had always wanted as well as a nice box of chocolates for my mum. The rest of the holiday went really well, and I returned to London on Friday a very happy young man.

This experience has taught me that ordinary miracles can happen every day. Guardian angels do exist and don't conform to the stereotype as portrayed in the movies. They come in all shapes and sizes and types of dress!

Chris Clavey

Cured of Cancer

My wife was diagnosed with multiple myeloma, cancer similar to leukemia where the body floods itself with white blood cells which lead to an unpleasant death. She was put on a type of chemo that, here in the US, cost $12,500 per month for four years.

I thank God that our insurance covered nearly all of it! After the four years on the chemo, the blood counts began to rise. Her doctors recommended a bone marrow transplant early to have a better chance of success. It was predicted to give her only an extra year and a half.

Following the transplant, the blood was clear, but it would return after the year or year and a half. Shortly after coming home the doctor called and wanted her to return! We were alarmed; why? When we met he said the European research on the disease showed a 2nd transplant done quickly after recovery from the first might increase her being free of the disease for up to three or three and a half years before returning.

Again, after the 2nd procedure, she was cancer free, but we knew the specialists had said it would return. She went back quarterly for a time, then every six months for blood work. Each time the doctor was pleased to report it had not come back yet. It's now been twelve years and the doctor always says, "There is no excuse for her to still be with us but –" and he points upward!

He added that her type of multiple myeloma is the most difficult to deal with and usually keeps coming back. He was amazed there were absolutely no cancerous or suspicious cells present and all blood chemical were perfectly normal.

I'm firmly convinced the only reason for this is Divine intervention and a Godly healing!

Jim Thomas

God's Perfect Timing

This is a miracle that reflects God's perfect timing when all does not seem to be going well.

I was heading towards the Crown Court to support my granddaughter, whom, along with some friends, was getting a man done for harassment. Outside of the court, dozens of people flooded in and out. It was very crowded and very busy. I suddenly looked over to the left, and everyone was gone, but coming up the stairs was my daughter, whom I had not been in touch with for over three years.

I was stunned and shaking. There was not a single soul around, everyone had gone! Yet, out of the blue, here was my daughter who had not spoken to me in three years, suddenly walking over to me, embracing and kissing me, as if nothing had ever happened to separate us!

To top that off, there had also not been any communication between us about the case, but here, the two of us were! When I got home, I fell to my knees and prayed, thanking God for allowing me to see my daughter!

This was meant to happen; no drama, no-one around, no nothing! It just happened!

Anonymous

A Message from God

I attended a prayer meeting at the Pentecostal church where everyone was given forty-five minutes to pray before we had a Bible discussion. Later in the prayer meeting, I was approached by a former missionary, who is now a pastor of the church. He was a very impassioned man who, when he led the service, gave incredible testimonies about God and the Holy Spirit.

He said to me, "The Holy Spirit has told me to tell you to let go of whatever is holding you back. God will give you joy, and power and love. The word 'Abba' means 'daddy'. God is your daddy, and he wants you to run to him and he will carry you on his shoulder."

He stopped speaking for a moment, and firmly placed his hand on my head and began speaking in tongues. I felt a gentle heat flow from the missionary, and I began feeling more content and peaceful.

He then said to me, "Chin up, when you walk, you walk with your head down. You need to be looking up! You have a destiny; God has given you a purpose. Let go of whatever is holding you back."

After a few moments, he then said, "You have a twinkle in your eyes, and you're smiling now! I don't even know you, but God has told me to come and tell you this!"

This feeling of contentment lasted with me for a while, and following this, I was getting on with my life as normal, I no longer felt as constrained as I did previously. I will always remember this, as a complete stranger came up to me, and suddenly made my life so much better from a simple prophecy!

Anonymous

Brian's Story of How They Met

Sometimes those who have family gatherings, family memories, and family ties don't realize what value there is in these things until you meet someone who has never known family.

I never knew sibling rivalry, family dinners, vacations, or family jokes. I never had the hugs, kisses, and structure of the family.

I was put up for adoption at a young age and was adopted by an abusive family in California. This eventually opened the door to a life on the streets when I was 12–13 years old. I don't speak much about those days. I spent time in mental institutions, on psyche meds, and in gangs, all the time filled with a gross darkness as the result of rejection, abandonment, and bitterness. I was not able to understand why my family would put me up for adoption, or why my adopted family abused me. And yet, in a strange way, these things – these needs – are what brought me to my Saviour, Jesus Christ. All the things done to me are now gone, covered and healed by the blood of Jesus.

I encountered God at an early age, long before I left home, but it wasn't until later in life that God manifested Himself to me in a way that changed my life forever.

This was the beginning of years which I spent praying, and seeking God for much, including healing from the pains and hurts of being a child given up for adoption.

Surrendering my life to God did not give me answers to my questions, such as, "Why did my folks abandon me?" But these questions about my family bothered me less. God was now my father and mother, leading and guided me through tough times, through rough waters, and fire to a better life.

I have now spent many years surrendered to God and I have seen many people healed, delivered and set free from bondage, by the power of the Holy Spirit. Blind eyes and deaf ears have been opened. I have heard the mute speak and seen the paralyzed walking; demons have been expelled and cancers healed as I preach on the streets of downtown Portland, Oregon.

Yet my ministering and pastoring in various churches could not prepare me for what was to come. This miracle that has happened is the greatest miracle he has ever witnessed. And if God can do this miracle for him, just think about the miracles that await you.

Many months ago, I did a DNA test through an online agency in the hope that the question, "Who is my family?" might be answered. I wondered what it would be like if someone responded, not wanting to get my hopes up. Days and months went by with no real contact from anyone.

Then the appointed day from God arrived. I received a message from a first cousin from Dayton, Ohio, who is also called "Brian."

Brian responded with a little excerpt of his life and suggested we meet up, which we did on March 19th, 2018.

People know that not all adoption stories or reunions end the same way. Some people meet but their heart's doors remain closed. Some are met with even more hurt and pain. But for me, what happened was something completely unexpected and wonderful beyond measure.

One of the first things I found out was that cousin "Brian" was named after me. His mother, Linda, was my aunt. She had raised me for eighteen months when I was very young until I was adopted. Linda gave me answers to my many questions. Not all the answers were pleasant, but they were answers nonetheless.

My mothers' name was Mary. She had a mental illness this led to the abuse. Linda told me of cigarette burns and a broken leg which led to my adoption. Linda had other news, too. Yes, I had siblings. I was the oldest at 42, but I have two brothers, and two sisters: Jamar, Justin, Michele, and Nisha. Our mother was unable to care for any of us because of her mental illness.

Hence, all the kids were put up for adoption. Jamar and Justin to one family. Michele and Nisha to another. I discovered that Jamar is an evangelist/street preacher active in his church, serving and loving God with his wife, and five children. Michelle, married, has two children. I haven't been able to locate Nisha and Justin yet.

Jamar said he had been looking for me for years but had very limited information to go on. Really, he had only what seems to be some sort of court papers documenting how we ended up being placed in adoptions.

Michelle, Jamar and I met up for the first time while video chatting through Facebook. I was overwhelmed, understandably. Jamar and Michelle had already been in contact with each other. But this was the first time all three of us had laid eyes on each other.

It felt extraordinary to hear my brother and sisters' voice for the first time, to see their faces. We started seeing the similarities in our looks and learned about our likes and dislikes. Sometimes, we were just quiet in awe at how God did this. We all felt, I think, that we were able to love and accept one another because we had been brought through our experiences by God.

I learned that my mother, Mary, had surrendered her life to Jesus Christ before passing away in 2015. What a great sense of peace to know that, after her life of turmoil and torment, she will one day see all of her children in heaven. She will be healed, whole and full of love.

Why are we reaching out? Because God is good and has moved in a way and in a time that seemed to come from nowhere. But we know He moved from eternity. He moved from love. He moved within answers to prayers.

I have been freed from the chains that long ago tried to bury me. The chains of resentment, unforgiveness, and rejection. I know I am absolutely 100% free and able to enjoy the fullness of this gift from God. There are no strings attached. There are no hidden agendas. There is nothing left undone to hinder building a relationship with the family I never knew.

Brian Chavarria

Faith in the Impossible

A miracle that I have encountered. I was involved in an accident that could have proved to be bad. I was driving my daughter's mother to the hospital while she was six months pregnant with our daughter. It was raining very hard. An approaching car at an unsafe and high-rate speed, attempted to pass us in those harsh conditions, and rear-ended us, causing the car to hydroplane.

The car spun out of control. It flipped and ejected my pregnant girlfriend out of the back window and into a wooded area. Although the accident induced the premature birth of our daughter, the three of us walked away with minor injuries, and my daughter has grown to become an amazing young woman!

I wondered whether our daughter would survive the complications that were ahead. She was born three months early and only weighed 1 pound 12 ounces. She was so tiny! And our positions as parents? We felt hopeless, but I knew deep down that our daughter would survive, and I wouldn't accept anything less.

I never doubted that our daughter would overcome any and all odds!

This event has guided me through some of my most difficult times. This has reaffirmed my faith in the impossible!

Anonymous

Double Healing

I've always had health problems and suffered from stomach issues all my life. When I was around twenty-two years old, I became very unwell with an ill stomach.

I had it for days and was both on the toilet whilst bent sideways over the bath, both vomiting and having a bad case of diarrhea. It was horrible, and I prayed and prayed earnestly, and said, "Why me God? Can you take this away from me?"

Within a few minutes of my thinking this, my stomach bug went away. I was no longer being sick, and diarrhea had stopped.

I pray to and worship a Living God!

Pauline Poppy

God's Protection

Seventeen years ago, I was diagnosed with breast cancer. I went through chemotherapy, which causes the immune system to become very weak and lose much of its resilience to illnesses and bacteria. Even the common cold or any minor illness could be far more severe than usual.

At this time, I was on holiday and was staying in a shared family house where some of the family members contracted a terrible virus. I had to be careful, as this could have been extremely harmful to me, given my health and immune system was already severely compromised from chemotherapy.

Everything was touch and go, and I wondered what God had planned for me, and where my journey in life would lead me. Despite all odds, I never contracted this virus which seemed an impossible miracle given how vulnerable my body was from chemo.

I believe in my heart God was protecting me, as there was no other explanation for me not contracting the virus. I also recovered from having breast cancer and am now living a happy and healthy life!

Anonymous

God Provides

It was at my local community center, in the Wednesday afternoon group called the Mayflower club. Most afternoons there's a speaker or a charity function going on, and that afternoon someone played the guitar and we just sang along. I remember that I did not know any of the songs they sang that day.

In my pockets, I gathered together all I had which was mostly copper coins and five pence pieces, totaling about forty pence. When the collection box was thrust in front of me, I reached into my pocket to retrieve the coins. As I released the coins, I realized they were all silver.

It seemed the two pence coins had turned into ten pence coins and the one pence coins became five pence coins. Then I reached into my pocket and all that was left was one two pence and a single one pence coin. All the rest was put into the charity box and had turned to silver coins!

To this day I view this as a miracle because the very little I had to put into the box and what I had had been multiplied five times!

Gabriella Palmer

A Cry of Desperation

Going back ten years, in 2008, I was an alcoholic. I was living in a flat above a computer business office. This office had once been mine, but after we suffered an armed robbery, we never recovered, and my business closed. One evening, it was terribly cold and raining heavily outside, I accidentally locked myself out of my flat. I was not dressed for the weather. I was freezing and in a desperate situation.

In my head, I began to question God's existence, and said, "God if you exist –"

At that moment, before I'd even finished what I was going to ask, He turned my head. I have no other explanation for it.

In one of the bushes was a ten-pound note. In my audacity and desperation, I had the nerve to question God on His existence, and here, he helped me in my time of need!

I bought a drink, and my brother dropped me off a spare pair of keys, so I could let myself in, and had another set cut. This event was pivotal in my life, as I went from being in a state of confusion to clarity! Every step after that became clearer. It was a major step forward in my recovery, and I am now no longer an alcoholic and am living life again. This event strengthened my belief in God, and I use this as an example for others to help strengthen their beliefs.

I will never question God again!

Ed Quasir

Healing Prayer

I suffered from back pain for many years. Although I was still able to walk my dog and get out and about all the time, at times the pain was dreadful. In September 2016, I had an operation on my back, to release the nerves, which was initially successful. I was able to get out and continue with my life as normal. Unfortunately, this cure was only temporary, and my back got worse again.

I struggled with getting around my house and had to use a Zimmer frame. My walking got worse, I was on painkillers, and I could no longer walk my dog like I used to and could not do what I did previously. At Christmas 2017, I went to my local church and spoke with Pastor James, who asked me to pray with him. He got on his knees and prayed for me, encouraging me to pray continuously for my need. I did just that – from that time I prayed continuously for healing.

By around February/March time, I was walking again! I slowly went from using a Zimmer frame to a walking stick to being able to walk without it! I can now get on with my life and am no longer in pain with my back! The operation was temporary, but in Jesus' name, I am healed! This healing involved no more hospital appointments and no more painkillers! It was God who heard my prayers; there is no other explanation! I turned sixty-eight on 29th July 2018, and I am feeling great!

David

An Incident

In 2003, I was diagnosed with lymphoma and was told by doctors that I only had four years left to live. I had to have my spleen removed, as it was about to burst, which would have ended my life there and then. A few weeks previously, before all of this happened, I had a falling accident.

I had slipped on some oil and was referred to A&E by my doctor. For months before all this happened, I had stomach pains and was unwell. I ignored it, as I thought it would pass. When I was in the hospital, I had blood tests, and that was when I learned I had lymphoma. The stomach pains and sickness feeling were down to this!

The amount of love that was shown to me when I was in the hospital was overwhelming! The doctors and nurses who cared for me were so loving and compassionate!

To me, that is something like a miracle, for if I had not slipped on the oil, I would have died many years ago. The second miracle is that I outlived what the doctors' predicted! It is now 2018, and I am alive and well!

Jean Parsons

My Healed Foot

A few years back, I had problems with my foot. I could not walk properly and had a limp. At that time, I was on a placement and was doing my NVQs. I had pulled my hamstrings, worsening my pain, and could not put my foot down. One of those days, I was out in my local village and was in so much pain that I went to my doctor who gave me two options.

He first showed me a huge needle which would have pumped a steroid into my leg to calm in the inflammation in my leg and foot. Secondly, he recommended me to have surgery, which was not always successful, and would have left me with a bad leg for the rest of my life!

I left the doctor, refusing both options, and went to my church. Once I was there, I spoke with my Pastor. He dropped to his knees and prayed for me. After two weeks I was feeling better, and after a month, I was totally healed! There was no more pain, and I was fine!

I believe in the healing power of Christ!

Ian

My Beautiful Son

My miracle was the birth of my beautiful son!

When I was younger, I used to starve myself, but my anorexia remained largely unnoticed by family members, as I wore baggy clothes to hide my bony figure. Throughout my life, I've also experienced a lot of negativity, and tough times.

When I was a teenager, I took an overdose. I was informed by doctors that due to my poor health and the drug overdose, I would not be able to conceive. Later in my life, there was one year that really put me to the test! Within the same year, I was raped, struggled to cope with family bereavement, was mugged, and someone broke into my parents' house whilst I was inside!

Despite all the emotional turmoil and chaos that I experienced, I yet managed to conceive and had a beautiful baby boy! The drug overdose, the anorexia, the difficult times just made me a stronger person, and to be told that I would never conceive did not matter!

I count my baby boy as my miracle!

Anonymous

Against All Odds

Twenty-two years ago, my son was born prematurely weighing just one pound fourteen ounces. He had gangrene of the stomach, kidney failure, his heart valve had to be tied as it was open, and he had numerous other health needs and required a multitude of operations.

Then God told me that he was going to live; against all the odds of the doctors saying that he would not make it. I felt God in my heart tell me that he would live! My son is now twenty-two, and is a very happy, healthy young man, with no health problems at all! He is also doing really well and getting on with his life!

Eddie Marsh

End of My Addictions

I used to be a drug addict, alcoholic and cigarette smoker. But on 7th September 2017, my life changed completely.

I was forty-six years old on that day, which was also my birthday. I had been praying to God to take away my addictions. I had been an addict for years, and I wanted to change. I said to God, "If You take my addictions, I will be a more honest man." In an instant, I was no longer addicted to alcohol, cocaine, meth, and cigarettes. I heard God say to me, "I want you to be The Light within the Darkness," referring, no doubt, to the darkness of my life. I was transformed at that moment!

God talks to me every single day. When He talks to me, it feels like a pair of hands on my head, and a physical energy of peace flow through me. Now, I work with people with addictions, complex mental health needs, and ex-offenders. I am one of the lights to other people.

At the end of the day, it is down to God to decide; it's always in God's hands. I am just His servant!

Eddie Marsh

From the Heart

Many years ago, my children had been put up for adoption by social services. I prayed and prayed that I would get them back, and they would come back to me. I begged God that He would let me have my children back. In my garden I had a greenhouse, and whilst I was praying, I had a vision.

In the vision, I could see some children coming towards me. I saw it again, only this time, I could see children playing in a greenhouse; the exact same greenhouse I had in my garden!

I later had my children sent back! The vision was God telling me that I would get my children back! I cannot explain it! I know in my heart that it was God's way of communicating with me that I would get my children back!

Nicola

Bad Dreams

One night I had a dream that I was shot in the leg with a bow and arrow. When I woke up, I had leg pains which worsened over the course of a few weeks, later realizing my leg was actually swollen and, it got to the point in which I could not move it. I went to the hospital, and the staff said there was nothing wrong, but the pains and swelling continued, and I could not play any sport for a while. I prayed and fasted, and I cried out to Jesus for healing. The pain and the swelling went away soon after! There is power in His Name! Put your trust in Him!

Obinagwam Emmanuel

Jesus My Saviour

God has answered many prayers for me. I survived a violent conflict following a property dispute with some 'Omoniles' (owners of a village) in Lagos, Nigeria.

I was buying some land to start my home, and a group of people formed an Omonile where I was purchasing. However, I later learned that these were jobless youths who claimed that they would pay money for each property on the land, but instead, ransacked the houses, demanded people pay them for properties and killed the people who refused to!

They would then resell the houses to other people without the owner's consent! At present in Southwest Lagos, there is an injustice against the people, where Omoniles are a threat to the people by ransacking and defrauding the people of their properties.

After two years of living in my property in Lagos, I had run out of money as my office and two shops had been destroyed, and I was out of work. Living on five cents a day with barely anything to eat, I turned to my Bible.

Philippians 4:19: "And my God will supply every need of yours according to his riches in glory in Christ Jesus." After reading this, I was asked if I could do some home maintenance and painting jobs for other people's properties in the area. God answered my prayers! I had some money and could support myself for a brief period.

My landlord then clamped down on me for not paying my rent and had all my belongings thrown out of the house. I called on Jesus again, and not long after my landlord had gone, members of my church came and took my property back to the church and stored everything, giving me time to sort things out.

I was praying to God, thanking Him for being there in my time of need. Not long after, I was approached by an Omonile as I came to the end of my prayers. A violent conflict burst out and I was shot in the side. It left a 2cm scar, but I was not seriously harmed. The gun was then pointed at my head and the trigger pulled.

No bullets came out and I was safe. The man dropped the gun and ran off. I recognized the gunman, as he'd seen me praying before. I believe the Lord saved me that day! I was almost killed with a bullet to the head! Praise Jesus!

Put your faith Jesus and He will meet all your needs!

Obinagwam Emmanuel

Back to the Cross

God took me on even though I had been a drug addict and an alcoholic brawler addicted to porn. I had an affair as a single man with a married woman, and I was an angry person who would cuss you out in a heartbeat.

I was a hateful bully. I was a billy-bad; a bar hopper who committed fornication constantly. One day, Jesus got a hold of me and changed my life. Now I'm a Spirit-filled preacher and I just want to tell people how much Jesus loves them and wants to give them so much more than the world could ever offer. Jesus said, "I am the way the truth and the life. No one comes to the Father except through me." (John 14:6)

So often people believe that repentance means that you're sorry for your sins; that is only part of it! People often they forget about the change in your ways, and that God has the power to change those things in your life that you can't do on your own.

Anonymous

You Are My Child

This happened when some years back before I went downhill with depression. I was trying to attend my Catholic church more and wanted to be more active in my faith. During the Mass, I was pondering on my life and thinking to myself, "Why am I here?" I was totally lost in my thoughts and wondering what was next for me.

Behind me, I suddenly felt a warm presence. I had no idea what it was! There was no one behind me, yet, what I felt was like a pair of warm arms descending upon me and wrapping themselves around me! It was a very overwhelming feeling. I felt powerless, but I also felt loved.

After the Mass, I spoke with the priest and told him about my experience. It was incredible! God wrapped His arms around me and comforted me in my time of need! Looking back on this, it was God's way of telling me, "Hang in there! You've got this! You are My Child."

Not long after this happened, I went downhill with massive depression, which was a terrible experience and struggle for me! This was God's way of telling me that I'd made it this far and to keep going!

Anonymous

Saved by a Prayer

It was in 1996 and was the most traumatic thing I have ever experienced!

I was at home with my 18-month-old granddaughter. I had had a bath, and wrapped the robe around me, and left my sleeping granddaughter on the bed. I thought I was home alone until I heard footsteps in my house. I was suddenly confronted with three African men.

They bound my head, tied my wrists and my ankles and strung me up against the wall.

One of them ransacked my house and pulled all the phone plugs out so no one could get in touch with me, one of them took a large kitchen knife and held it to my throat, and the third drew all the curtains in the house so no one could see in.

One of them, using the palm of his hand, began to repeatedly hit my head against the wall. I kept my head low and refused to look up.

I prayed, "Our Father" very quietly, and also asked them to not hurt my granddaughter.

I was beyond the stage of fear; I could not scream. I was staring death in the face. Earlier this year, my mum had passed, and my son's first wife was killed in a car crash. Mentally, I began having a conversation saying, "Mum, Kate. I may get to see you again soon."

I summoned up the courage to ask them, as calmly as I could, to not hurt my granddaughter. I was still praying, "Our Father." I began saying it softly.

The man who was repeatedly hitting me told me to "shut up!" I did not.

One of the men asked me, "Where is the money safe?" The knife was to my throat and I was still praying. I quietly replied, "There is a money bag in the front room."

One of the men took a pair of trousers, put it over my head and tied the legs around my neck. I was picked up by two others and laid on the bathroom floor. In that instant, I thought I was going to die. I was still praying.

The men walked out. I listened as their footsteps became more and more distant until a dead silence gripped my flat. I lay quietly and heard one of the men come back. I could feel his shadow cast over me. I heard a hushed whisper say, "Shame. Shame."

He then left, and a haunting silence took over.

Once I knew that he was gone, I wriggled out of the bathroom and struggled with getting my wrists and ankles untied. Once I managed to, I checked my sleeping grandchild, who was unhurt! I then reconnected my phone, called my son, my husband and the police who all came immediately.

My house was completely empty. They had taken everything.

A few days later, a man was walking down my driveway. In my gut, I knew that he was one of the three. He knocked on the door and gave me an apology.

"I am sorry, Madam."

He proceeded to tell me that the robbery was a set up by a woman I know and that he knew where my stolen property was. I phoned the police, who arrived in an army truck, and he guided us to the township.

After the police put him in camouflage gear and a balaclava (as this would have cost him his life if his partners found out he turned them in) he pointed out the house where my property was.

The lady I knew lived there. She was gone without a trace. No-one knew where she had gone.

Around the corner from where I stood, a child came cycling round on my grandsons' stolen bike.

There were two miracles that took place over the course of these events.

The first was that I survived and am still doing well today! The second is the change of heart that that man had. The fact that despite everything he did, he came back, apologized, and helped me to get my property back!

I attest these miracles through ceaseless prayer!

Anonymous

God Hears Us

I was about seventeen at that time. I was in Sixth Form College and I was doing an individual project on Human Trafficking. As part of my studies for this project, I watched documentaries, read articles, and contacted different charities for information to aid my understanding and for more insight into how to tackle this problem.

I found myself at times very emotional because of the case studies I would read, that would leave me in a tearful mess. My heart always went out to those who had been trafficked, and I felt so helpless reading the horror stories of cases that I would find when doing research.

I could not bear the thought of young children and women being forced into sexual servitude, and to be used and grossly mistreated by people who only cared about money. The thought of it devastated me; I was enraged by the people who dehumanizing others in such a way!

One evening, I was at home typing up some of my work, and I was saddened by some heart-breaking images of children who had been trafficked. Their freedom had been taken from them, and their lives plunged into a black hole of slavery, misery and mistreatment, all for profit. I began to pray.

Warm tears rolled down my cheeks, and in my heart, I begged God that something would be done to save those who had been trafficked. I prayed that He would touch the hearts of the traffickers, so that they may see the devastation they are causing, and that the women and children who are trafficked are human beings, not property.

On my laptop screen, a news link flashed. It was a news release of what was happening across the globe. I could not believe my eyes! The largest trafficking ring in China had been destroyed! Over three hundred girls had been rescued and over one hundred arrests had been made!

In my heart, I knew that God intended for me to see this news link. This miracle for me not only gave me joy for the three hundred girls who had been rescued but also because it reminded me of what a powerful thing it is for us to pray from the heart.

If you truly pray from the heart, God will hear you and he will comfort you, and answer your prayer in the most wondrous of ways! Praise the Lord!

Anonymous

Saved by Grace

I grew up in small-town Alabama (US). I'm from a very poor, dysfunctional family of six children, headed by my sadistic father. My Father, a chronic alcoholic and addict, a notorious outlaw, loved to see others in pain. God was never spoken about in my household unless I was visiting my devout Christian grandmother.

My father had a terrible string of criminal convictions, starting when he was nine after being incarcerated for running away and his involvement in an armed robbery of a gas station. Others included having shootouts with the police.

My mother was from Georgia, from a very poor bootlegging family of Cherokee descent.

She never drank or used drugs but did attempt suicide to escape the evil man that my father was.

I was afraid of him. Many days and nights of fear dominated my childhood.

We lived in a four-room shack with no running hot water. We bathed at the creek or under a garden hose, or a washtub in front of a heater. Everything from robbing jewelry stores and post offices to armed bank robberies, that's what my father did.

Once, my daddy shot an apple off of my brother John's head from a lengthy distance with a pistol. Yes, my childhood was not a fairy tale, nor was it happy. My family and my God knows. He even sold my eldest brother T. Mac as a baby. My mother got straight on a Greyhound bus to Detroit to get her son back. Little T.Mac grew up to be a preacher and has preached the Gospel since the age of 18. He is now 64.

On August the 8th 1976 I witnessed my Dad and his long-time crime associate in a brawl. My dad took out his pistol and shot his friend seven or eight times in the stomach.

My mother phoned the police. My daddy was in a disorientated state in the house. He was drunk. Once the police arrived, he attempted to open fire on them but was shot fatally. He was killed in his Sunday suit minus his tie and coat. Shot in the mouth by police with a .357 mag.

My mother ran screaming outside. Only the Lord saved her from being fatally wounded. My father lay dead in the driveway from a little after nine until midnight or so. I watched the coroner wrap gauze around his fingers and take the body away.

This was when my own saga of running from God began. I hated Him. God wasn't spoken in our home unless in the wrong way – except by my praying, witnessing, God-fearing granny.

31 years later, in 2007, I cried out to God and surrendered to Him. After years of confusion, darkness, and being totally lost after my traumatic childhood, God spoke to me. I heard Him say, "You are Mine."

The Lord God Almighty is alive upon the throne today forevermore. And I am a blood-bought child of the King by way of Calvary's Cross through Jesus Christ our Lord. Salvation comes by way of Calvary.

Praise God for my praying granny and all the praying saints of God. Mother is now deceased, but all six children are living and are very much alive in Christ. Glory Hallelujah Praise the name of the Lord!

My testimony is this: if you pray continually, and if you let God use you for His plan, you will accomplish more than you realize despite the circumstances.

Anonymous

In the Palm of Jesus' Hand

Today, I sit and think of the wonderful, miraculous work that the Lord performed in my life. It wasn't that long ago while living in Gillits, Durban, that Angela and I were taking care of her family. Her sister was unemployed, and we were the only ones at the time able to give them assistance. So we rented a house which was far more than we required and we all moved in together.

During this time, it was my function to take and fetch Holly, my niece, from school in Kloof and I did this every day without incident for some time. However, one particular afternoon, just before I left to pick her up, I realized that I had not taken my medication to prevent seizures. So I took a tablet with the intention of taking a second one upon my return.

Anyway, I got into my car to go and pick her up and after being on the road for about five minutes I began to feel the feelings I get before I have a seizure. I took a turn with the intention to pull over to the side of the road until it passed and at the same time I shouted out, "Lord Jesus help me!" Before I was able to pull over the seizure took full effect and I lost consciousness.

This was virtually a minute or two from the school. Well, someone drove my car for twenty-five minutes and no one can do that but the Lord or one of His angels that He sent to take care of me. I have no idea where the car was driven for those twenty-five minutes, but do you know how far you can drive for that period of time without having an accident, driving on the correct side of the road and at the correct speed?

Why I say this is that because I came to twenty-five minutes later on the correct side of the road driving past the high school which is on the other side of where I needed to go and driving at the correct speed. I immediately headed towards the primary school to pick Holly up. She had gone back into the school to the Headmaster's office to wait for me. The very strange thing about all this is that I had not fully understood what had happened until I got home with Holly. It was only then that I realized what the Lord had done for me and how He had undertaken for me. I share this real-life event with you to give glory to the Lord God Almighty and to testify of His majesty and to give Him praise and honor.

I also testify that every single word I have written is absolutely true. He is such a great and gracious God and how I absolutely thank Him for holding me in the palm of His hand even as His Word confirms!

Michael Dudley Roodt

Miracle Baby

An amazing miracle happened in my family, five years ago in 2013. My daughter-in-law at that time had one daughter, aged 4. She and her husband desired another child, but she could not conceive. They attempted IVF three times, but still no success. It was a truly heart-breaking time for them.

My husband and I went to visit them. I chatted with my daughter-in-law for a bit, and she said that she would not try IVF again as it was too upsetting for her. I told her that I would pray for her, that she would be able to conceive naturally.

Her reply was that it would not happen. It was just not possible. I told her that I would still pray nonetheless, as nothing is impossible with God. Each day following this conversation, I prayed and spoke with God that she would be able to conceive and be blessed with a child.

Around two months later, she received a phone call to say that she was pregnant! Seven months later, she gave birth to a beautiful baby girl! Praise and glory to God!

Luke 1:37 "For nothing will be impossible with God."

Anonymous

Walk Again

This was something I witnessed when I was thirteen years of age and was the first miracle I ever witnessed. I was attending an Evangelist Conference, and the preacher asked anyone in the room if they wanted to be prayed for. I remember there was a man at the front of the room. He had withered legs that were folded. He could not walk and was physically severely disabled.

He asked the preacher for prayers, and the preacher did so. Whilst the preacher was praying, others in the room began to congregate around him, and all participate in a group prayer for him. There was some noise from the crowd that congregated around him, and I went closer to see what was happening.

Suddenly, this man who could not walk, whose legs were withered and folded, began to unfold and he started to walk, very slowly! This was the most profound healing miracle that I ever witnessed as a boy! I watched a man who could not walk, suddenly get up and walk, at the power of prayer of the preacher and congregation!

Anonymous